Rainforest Biome

Mediterranean Biome

Outdoor Biome

Core

The Zigzag

Visitor Centre

Biome entrance

Link

Stage

0.01
0.02
0.03
0.04
0.05
0.06
0.07
0.08
0.09
0.10
0.11
0.12
0.13
0.14
0.15
0.16
0.17
0.18
0.19
0.20
0.21
0.22
0.23
0.24
0.25
0.26
0.27
0.28
0.29
0.30

D0191917

# Contents

Welcome to Eden. This guide gives a flavour of all the different sorts of things we do. For more information come and explore, visit the website, get involved in some of our projects and have a chat with some of the Eden team.

## Your tour guide

# Welcome

Eden is ten years old. It seems like a lifetime ago that we were dreaming and working in a small shed, first at the Lost Gardens of Heligan and then at Watering Lane Nursery. Sometimes I feel nostalgic and go and sit in the shed and dream a little more.

To be called a dreamer is usually either a gentle rebuke or a scoff, yet almost all the things I love are the products of dreaming. Oddly, many of them were dreamed up in a shed, that simple wooden retreat with a view. Henry Ford dreamed motor cars, Steve Jobs computers; many of the world's favourite novels, plays and film scripts owe their existence to sheds and an extremely large number of scientific and engineering breakthroughs likewise. I wonder if as many dreams have come to fruition in magnificent marble and chrome buildings?

17 March 2011 marked our tenth birthday, by which time we had welcomed 12.8 million visitors, grown the largest rainforest in captivity, created 520 full-time jobs at Eden, formed working relationships with thousands of local suppliers and those that source sustainably from further afield, and helped economic regeneration in Cornwall. We've built the Biomes and Core using sustainable construction techniques, created a Waste Neutral programme, started renewable energy projects and are working on collaborative projects exploring ways of living in the 21st century. And that's just for starters. Not bad for a shared dream!

Thank you for your support over the past ten years, and we look forward to sharing the years ahead with you.

# What Eden is all about

The 21st century will present enormous challenges to our society: food security, energy security, population growth and movement, all cranked up by climate change. That's the end of the gloom and doom bit, because Eden is about demonstrating the art of the possible, like building this place in a hole in the ground – more later.

Our site displays and celebrates ways in which our world supports us all. (Note 'our' – the world would carry on very nicely without us.) We also explore ways in which we can look after our world in return. It's not just about conservation, it also involves repairing things we've messed up, re-inventing the world we have made, working with and above all respecting nature.

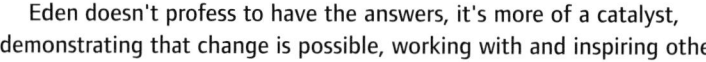

Eden doesn't profess to have the answers, it's more of a catalyst, demonstrating that change is possible, working with and inspiring others.

There's no rule book for a successful future, so imagination, creativity and enterprise are needed to try to find new solutions. Humans have the wit and ability to do all this. We just need to explore the kind of people we want to be, the kind of society we want to build, and harness and cultivate the talents and skills to get there. And it's going to be a darn sight easier if we all work together; a collective response showing the possibilities for living in the 21st century; a call to action. Want to get involved?

## The Eden Project is an educational charity

Where does the money go? On public education right here for everyone and towards our projects, as described throughout this guide. Thank you for your support.

The pit is filled with exhibits and events showing our dependence on the natural world and each other – inspiring and encouraging us all to care about these things.

Our extensive palette of projects explores how we can adapt to new ways of living – demonstrating what can be achieved when people work together and with nature.

We built our HQ in an old china clay pit to demonstrate regeneration – a symbol of positive change.

## That's what Eden is about!

*Extreme gardening*

*Eden projects*

# If you believe

*there should be a place that explores what a great future might look like,*

*that celebrates life and puts champagne in the veins,*

*that's all about education with Mud Between Your Toes,*

*that is a place where you can hold conversations that might just go somewhere,*

*where research is experience to be shared with everyone,*

*and is for all those who think the future belongs to us all,*

*then welcome to the Eden Project, home of the Eden Trust.*

*That's why we built this place and that's where the money goes.*

*Events*

*Exhibits, education, exploration*

# The natural world – our life support system

## Resources

We sow, grow and exhibit plants for: food, fuel, medicine, materials, beauty, music, sport, entertainment … to show our dependence on the green things of life. We show our reliance on minerals and metals too; after all, we do live in an old mine. Stories across the site tell of land use, people and systems worldwide that keep us all alive and kicking.

## Services

Exhibits reflect the world's wild places too. Forests, oceans, steppe and savannah act as air conditioners, water purifiers, waste recyclers, carbon capturers and climate controllers. These are called ecosystem services – similar to the services we have in our homes except they're free and vital for our survival. We're messing them up, which will land us in trouble if we don't do something about it.

*The Plant Takeaway – aka Dead Cat, Visitor Centre. Discover what happens when the plants we use are taken away.*

*Exhibits exploring services and projects addressing challenges, The Core (p.35).*

*Comfort and Mary, cocoa growers, travel worldwide sharing their stories of Fairtrade and Divine Chocolate as part of the Ghanaian Kuapa Kokoo co-operative.*

# We also depend on each other

Our exhibits, events and projects are about people using plants, growing crops and nurturing environments, evolving skills for survival, exploring how we need each other, working together, demonstrating things we have in common worldwide – far more than what separates us.

*Our winter programme with skating, skill-sharing, gift-making, processions, music, singing and dance celebrates community, collaboration, sharing and mutual support. Where people offer these valuable gifts to each other, resilient communities develop.*

# Eden's projects

Here is a flavour of some of the projects we're working on at Eden – working together, exploring how we can adapt to new ways of living. There are masses more: take a look through the Guide, on site and at **edenproject.com/whats-it-all-about**.

With all our projects we keep the following in mind:

Hope – an understanding that it's possible.

Collaboration – more heads are better than one.

Imagination and enterprise – exploring new ways of doing things.

Your support helps us turn our ideas into action. Thank you.

## Projects for Places

**– new landscapes, new lives**

The Eden story epitomises the power and possibilities of landscape restoration. We're working with the Cornish community on projects in our neighbourhood. Further afield, we're involved with restoration projects in the rainforests (p.40), on other post-mining sites (p.33) and in vulnerable island communities worldwide (p.42).

## Projects for People – building stronger communities

Communities with strong connections – that support, trust and believe in each other – can move mountains.

### The Big Lunch

Celebrate your neighbours by having lunch with them – in your street, park, playground, communal garden, home, anywhere – sharing food and conversation. Sunday

5 June 2011. Next year, Sunday 4 June 2012, the Big Lunch expands across the Commonwealth for the Queen's Diamond Jubilee celebrations. **thebiglunch.com**

# Projects for People – **harnessing and cultivating talents and skills**

Projects with communities, businesses, schools, colleges, the vulnerable and the excluded ...

## Eden Talent

Engaging people in their own life adventure, taking action through the world of work. Growing a motivated, better-informed workforce equipped with the skills needed for the 21st century with a clear role in society. We run programmes for local businesses (Green Foundation, p.17) and young people (Green Talent, p.21).

## Growing for Life

Supports the growing of food by prisoners, and assists ex-offenders, those at risk of offending or hard to reach, by providing horticultural training and qualifications through social businesses in the community.

# Projects for Climate – **Climate Revolution**

We explore what can be done about climate change individually and collectively, and what we need to know more about, including education around climate change, mitigation (reducing its effects) and adaption (changing how we live in response to it).

## Sexy Green Shows

Exhibit the funky new technology that is going into new low-carbon products that minimise the amount of greenhouse gases going into the air, changing the way we think about buying cars, houses and all the other stuff.

## 21st-Century Living

Explored what people found easy to do and what they found more tricky when going green in their homes. This research helps inform our exhibits programme and other projects such as:

## Clear About Carbon

Helping businesses understand more about the low-carbon economy and how they can work towards it. **clearaboutcarbon.com**

## The Pod

A web-based schools programme on sustainable futures. **jointhepod.org**

# A bit of history – regeneration

*'Between 1996 and 1998 a group of people gathered in pubs, hotels, private houses, offices and even motorway service stations to talk about an idea – to create a place like nothing anyone had ever seen before; a place that explored human dependence on plants and the natural world; a place that demonstrated what could be done if people who wanted to make a difference got together. It was ridiculous to imagine it was possible, it was ridiculous to imagine that hundreds of people trained to say no could be persuaded to say yes. But the greybeards had a brilliant plan: ask the youngsters to do it – they don't know it can't be done.'*  Tim Smit

Eden began as an act of regeneration, of land and people.

We bought an exhausted, steep-sided clay pit 60 metres deep, the area of 35 football pitches, with no soil, 15 metres below the water table, and gave it life: soil made from 'waste' materials, water harvested from the rain, giant conservatories and buildings that drew inspiration from nature. We populated it with a huge diversity of plants (ones we use every day but don't often get to see) and people from all walks of life and built within it structures and infrastructures.

We opened our Visitor Centre in 2000 so the public could watch the construction and share the adventure. We opened the whole site on 17 March 2001.

The Eden Project was established as one of the Landmark Millennium Projects to mark the year 2000 in the UK.

**The early 90s** While Tim Smit was restoring the Lost Gardens of Heligan he realised that plants could be made far more interesting by weaving human stories around them, tales of adventure, emotion and derring-do. There was a big story to be told … so he enlisted the help of his horticultural director, Philip McMillan Browse, and trustee/horticultural historian Peter Thoday: 'Let's make a list of the plants that changed the world.'

The list, a very long one, arrived: 'Here you go, you're going to need a very big conservatory.' A summer sunset on a china clay tip conjured thoughts of ancient civilizations in volcanic craters, and of putting the largest greenhouses in the world in a huge hole. Why not?

**1994** Restormel, our local Borough Council at that time, took a leap of faith, put up the first £25,000 and gave the story a beginning.

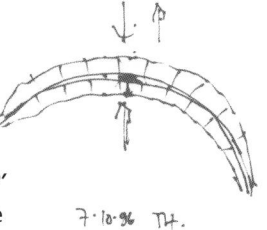

**1995** The good news for Grimshaw Architects: 'Would you like to build the eighth wonder of the world?' The bad: 'We don't have any money.' Grimshaws took the baton from Cornish architect Jonathan Ball (co-founder of the Project) and designed our fabulous buildings. (We paid them in the end!) The McAlpine Joint Venture worked for 18 months without payment or contract and

*The first Biome sketch, 1996, in the pub, on the proverbial napkin.*

then loaned Eden a significant sum only to be repaid if the Project was successful. This risk-sharing broke down the traditional barriers between designers and contractors and created a team dedicated to one vision.

Why did they do this? Because they wanted to change something and because they wanted to say, 'I'm glad I did,' rather than, 'I wish I had.'

Sounds simple? Not really. We were turned down by the Millennium Commission the first time we applied, and many left good jobs before we had raised a bean – or found a site. When our reworked bid secured £37.5m from the MC (huge thanks MC), we had to match fund to the tune of 50%. For the next 5 years a small team worked tirelessly (mainly in a shed) to turn the idea into a plan and into reality. Finance Director Gay Coley (MD from 2000) came on board to raise the money, fledgling teams grew thousands of plants, mapped them on to the site, started planning the stories … Oh, and we recruited a (pretty unique) team to run the place and made sure as well as having a good idea and a fabulous theatre that we had the ability to run it operationally. For the full story, read Tim Smit's *Eden* and visit **edenproject.com**.

The first sod was cut on 15 October 1998.

## The biggest sandpit in the world

To make the site better suited to people than to mountain goats we sliced 17 metres off the top to put in the bottom. 1.8 million tonnes were shifted in 6 months. Dodgy slopes were shaved to a safe angle and terraces created. Two thousand rock anchors, some 11 metres long, were driven into the pit sides to stabilise them, and a 'soup' of plant seed and fertiliser was sprayed on the slopes to knit the surface together.

## Soil

We started with none, and with help from Reading University, made over 83,000 tonnes – we didn't want to take it from elsewhere. The mineral part came from mine wastes: sand (IMERYS china clay) and clay (WBB Devon Clays Ltd). In the Biomes, composted bark provided long-lived organic matter. The Rainforest Biome plants needed a rich organic soil that could hold water and nutrients, while the slower growers in the drier Mediterranean Biome used a sandier mix. A nutrient-free mix was used in the South African Fynbos, where fertile soil is toxic to some of the plants. Outdoors, we used composted domestic green wastes. The soils were mixed (by a JCB) in a nearby china clay pit. Worms were added to help dig and fertilise.

We got into the *Guinness Book of Records* for using the most scaffolding, 230 miles of it – sorry to anyone who was needing some that year.

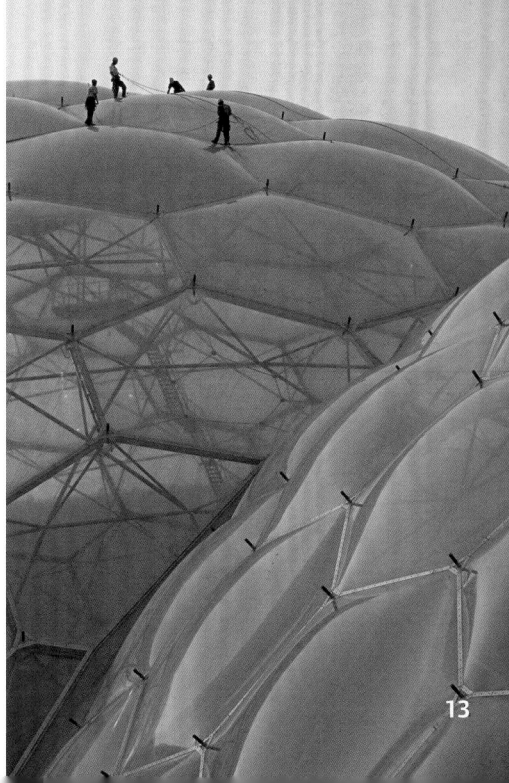

# The covered Biomes

The Biomes are the biggest conservatories in the world. Building these 'lean-to greenhouses' on an uneven surface was tricky: 'bubbles' were used because they can settle on any shaped surface.

**Overall design** Two-layer, curved space frame, 'the hex-tri-hex', with an outer layer of hexagons (the largest 11 metres across), plus the odd pentagon, and an inner layer of hexagons and triangles bolted together. The steelwork weighs only slightly more than the air contained by the Biomes. They are more likely to blow away than down, so are tied into the foundations with ground anchors (giant tent pegs).

**Transparent foil 'windows'** Ethylenetetrafluoroethylenecopolymer (ETFE): three layers, inflated 2-metre-deep pillows, lifespan over 25 years, transmits UV light, non-stick, self-cleaning. They weigh less than 1% of the equivalent area of glass, but can take the weight of a car.

**Climate** Monitored and controlled automatically. The main heating source is the sun, the back wall acts as a heat bank releasing heat at night, triple-'glazed' windows for insulation, air handling units to cool on hot days and heat on cool ones.

**Rainforest Biome** Misters create 90% humidity, irrigation from ground-level pipes.

**Mediterranean Biome** Drier; even in cooler periods the vents often open to reduce humidity and fungal problems.

*The pillows were installed by 22 professional abseilers – the sky monkeys.*

# The plants

Many were grown from seed in our nursery; others came from botanic gardens, research stations and supporters, mostly in Europe and the UK.

**Pollination** Some plants are insect-pollinated, some wind-pollinated, some paintbrush-pollinated! We do this when we need the flowers to produce seeds.

*Sulawesi White-eye*

**Pest and disease control** Our rigorous healthcare programme starts with isolation houses at Eden's nursery to catch pest and disease problems before they reach the site.

On site our integrated pest management system uses cultural methods (removal of infested plant parts), 'soft' chemicals (soaps and oils) and biological control (bugs that eat bugs). Spot the little bamboo pots on pulley systems which give the bugs a ride to the treetops. We also have some birds and lizards in the Biomes which eat their fill of pests. Our UV lightboxes catch pests and monitor their numbers.

## Extreme Gardening

Our Green Team (of 55, including science and knowledge transfer teams, landscape, nursery and on-site gardeners) often plant on near-vertical banks; have planted millions of plants of around 5,000 taxa; plant over half a million bulbs every autumn; plant around 60,000 new plants annually; start at 7.30 every day to prune and water before you arrive; do 50 hours weeding a week in the summer; remove about 25m³ of green waste from the site every week; recycle this material to make over 120 tonnes of compost a year.

Rainforest trees are pruned by abseilers, from a cherry picker and a Canopy Balloon (p.41); plants are propagated in our own nursery, we keep a record of every plant on site and have a large seed library.

Find tips from our Extreme Gardening Green Team on **edenproject.com/blog**

> *'If you want to go quickly, go alone.*
> *If you want to go far, go together.'*
>
> **African proverb**

Sustainable development is the ability to keep going and evolve in a changing world, taking into account **people**, the **planet** and **profits with a purpose** (the triple bottom line). It begins with an awareness of what we dare not lose and what we must work with to create a viable society in the 21st century. Massive social and environmental change, contributions to carbon reduction, energy security, food security, conservation, building communities that can cope – it all fits together.

## People

Eden has grown from 5 staff to over 500, plus 300 volunteers. Teams report to the Board, who report to the Trust, who ensure the operation meets its charitable aims. Art, science, horticulture, education, management, retail, catering, philosophy, economics, design, construction, publishing, research, housekeeping, stewarding, guiding, fundraising, storytelling, marketing, media – between them the team cover all these bases and more as we explore how to manage Eden as efficiently and sustainably as possible. What we grow, cook and sell, the way we operate and the projects we run, all explore ways of living in the decades to come.

We don't reproduce what others already do well, but collaborate, and often bring unlikely bedfellows together for conversations that just might go somewhere.

# Working with the local community

We run a wide range of community projects across Cornwall.

## Inspiring communities

Provides creative engagement and inspiration to help communities develop ideas and opportunities here and now for the future.

## A Great Day Out

Offers inspirational Eden vists to socially excluded groups who would not otherwise be able to experience what we have to offer. **edenproject.com/greatdayout**

## Green Foundation

Helps Cornish businesses to make the most of opportunities presented by the transition to a low-carbon economy.

**greenfoundation.org.uk**

## Eden Project Café

Brings a little bit of Eden to St Austell town centre with a distinctive quirky touch, and ethical and environmental credentials. Delicious fresh local food and drink, a space for arts exhibitions, music and community group meetings, and innovative fruit, veg and book swap schemes.

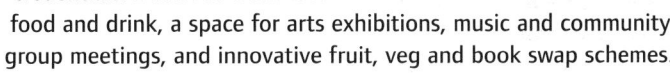

## Planet

We're committed to reducing our carbon footprint, using resources efficiently, generating our own renewable resources and being self-sufficient in soil, water and energy where possible.

### Efficiency

The Biomes' hexagons copy nature's honeycombs: maximum strength, minimum materials. Our construction programme sets high standards for good building design and process, and demonstrates the worth of natural materials and structures. Since 2008 we've reduced energy consumption by 6.5% and gas use by 20%. Our energy efficiency investment programme, including new control systems, boilers, lighting, etc (thanks partly to an interest-free loan from the Carbon Trust), should see us reduce our $CO_2$ emissions by 25% in two years.

Waste Neutral: we reduce, re-use and recycle our waste wherever possible (currently recycling 19 different waste streams) and we reinvest by purchasing items that are made from recycled materials.

### Switching to cleaner technologies

Photovoltaic panels on the Core roof and a small wind turbine generate clean electricity, while a biomass boiler (still with a few teething problems) partly replaces our gas system.

Nearly half our water needs – averaging 20,000 bathfuls a day – are provided from grey water harvested on site by a subterranean drainage system. We use it to irrigate our plants and flush our loos, while rainwater that falls on the Biomes is used to create the mist inside the Rainforest Biome. The Land Train uses waste vegetable oil bio-diesel. Our 'in-vessel' composter has turned 100 tonnes of food waste and 34 tonnes of green waste and other compostable material into 40 tonnes of plant compost for use on-site.

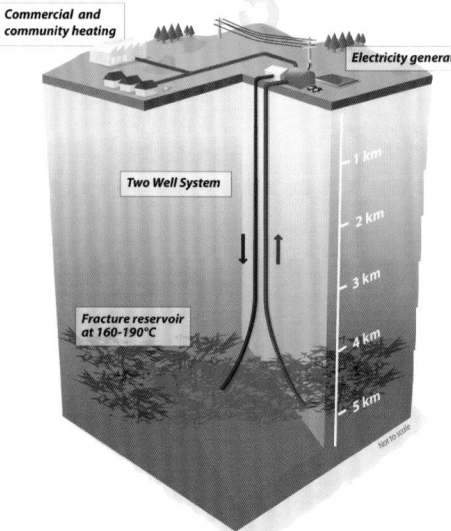

Commercial and community heating

Electricity generation

Two Well System

Fracture reservoir at 160-190°C

1 km
2 km
3 km
4 km
5 km

Not to scale

We're working up plans with EGS Energy Ltd, Penzance, for a deep geothermal power plant to supply Eden with zero-emission electricity and heat. Excess power (enough for around 3,500 households) will go to the National Grid. More on this and our energy policy and action plan at **edenproject.com/energy**.

## More $CO_2$ reductions

Low food miles, seasonal and vegetarian dishes all help reduce greenhouse gas emissions. Our tens of thousands of plants sequester carbon every day.

A green travel plan gives discounted entry to walkers, cyclists and those with combined coach, bus or rail tickets. Over 10% of visitors don't come by car and 35% of staff car-share or come by other means: not bad for a rural site!

We offset all our direct emissions, electricity and business travel through ClimateCare. The Eden Climate Fund invests through ClimateCare in projects in developing countries that reduce carbon in the atmosphere, and through Climate Revolution in climate-related education programmes and initiatives. You can help by donating to the Fund. **edenproject.com/climatefund**

## Profits with a purpose

Eden is a social enterprise, doing business to give the greatest possible benefit to the widest number of people and showing that improving the environment and livelihoods and building stronger communities can work hand in hand.

Since 2001 Eden's 12.8m visitors have helped us put over a billion pounds into the regional economy through year-round trade with local suppliers and businesses.

Over 80% of the money we spend on catering goes to Cornish suppliers. We work with local growers and companies to develop products for sale.

Fairtrade, organic and other certified products from further afield demonstrate that good trade is a vital part of sustainability too.

Nature:
planet—environment

Who decides
how to balance all
this? We all do.

Economics:
profits with
a purpose

Society: people —
working together

> *'You never change things by fighting the existing reality. To change something, build a new model that makes the existing model obsolete.'*
> R. Buckminster Fuller (1895–1983), architect, designer, visionary

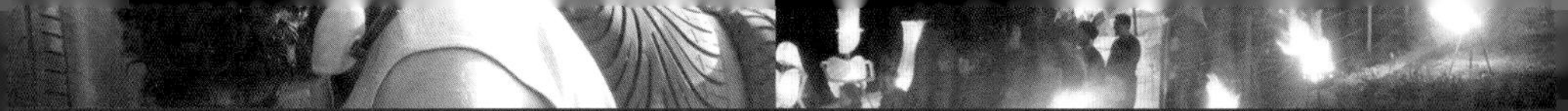

# Communication and public education

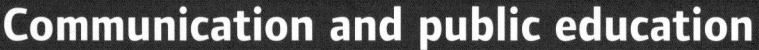

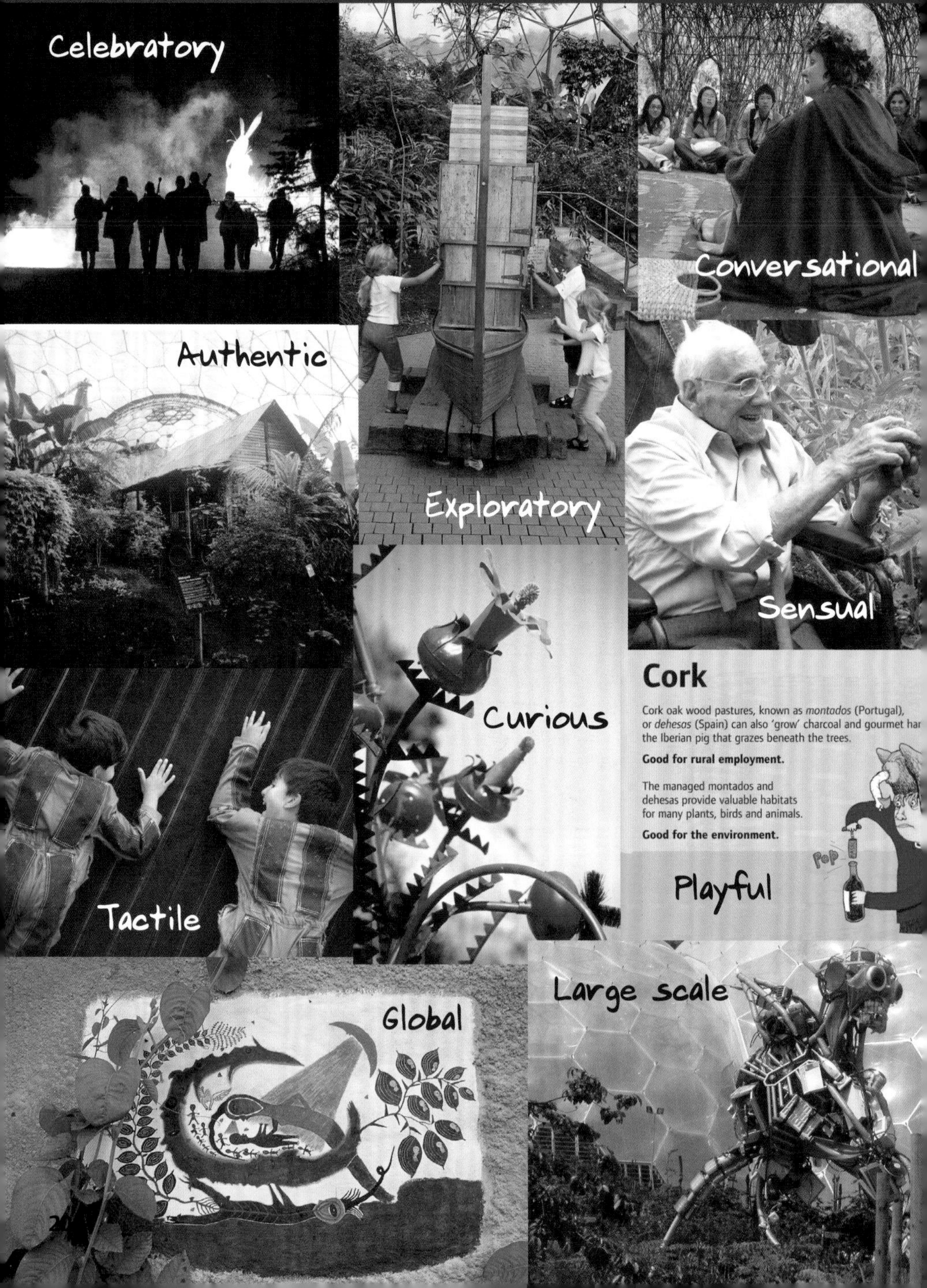
Celebratory
Conversational
Authentic
Exploratory
Sensual
Curious
Cork
Cork oak wood pastures, known as montados (Portugal), or dehesas (Spain) can also 'grow' charcoal and gourmet har the Iberian pig that grazes beneath the trees.
Good for rural employment.
The managed montados and dehesas provide valuable habitats for many plants, birds and animals.
Good for the environment.
POP
Playful
Tactile
Global
Large scale

## We love stories

*'Story is a powerful means of captivating, providing insight, testing moral choices, painting possible futures, challenging and holding a mirror up in a way that is acceptable – personal and impersonal at the same time. Unless a culture has strong stories it loses its direction. Eden aspires to be a place where the stories of our future are created and told – the Aesop's Fables of the 21st century.'*

Dr Tony Kendle, Eden Project

**The Pollination Team** Performers, guides, storytellers, internal communicators.

**The Artists** Helping to create 'signposts' to new attitudes and ways of thinking.

**The Creative Design Team** An in-house crew of graphic designers, designer-makers and live events programme producers.

**The Sensory Trust** Finding creative approaches to physical access and information sharing for all. **sensorytrust.org.uk**

## Learning programmes for schools and colleges

Our schools programme hosts over 45,000 young people a year from the UK and a further 10,000 from overseas. We're reconnecting young people with science – spot young explorers on a 'Crazy Chef Challenge', trekking round the world to find ingredients for the ultimate global cake, and intrepid travellers in 'Don't Forget Your Leech Socks' trying their survival skills in the Rainforest. **edenproject.com/schools**

**Green Talent** Linking the talent and skills of young people to the environmental challenges of the 21st century and their future jobs and careers. **greentalent.org** Case studies on **realcoolfutures.com**

We host over 10,000 further and higher education students annually. Topics include: sustainable construction, horticulture, agriculture, leisure and tourism, geography, climate change, environment and continuing professional development for teachers. **edenproject.com/schools-and-colleges/tertiary**

Do our programmes make a difference? Our in-house research team, in collaboration with Exeter University, evaluates them and shares the results.

# Planning your day

## The Stage

The home of our seasonal events programme (p.58)

## Outdoor Biome

Ten years ago this Biome (with the sky for a roof) was a barren landscape, with no soil and no plants. Find crops that provide your foods, fuels, medicines and materials, and discover how they have shaped your world. Imagine how things could change in the future. Explore our wild places too and consider why we need to conserve them.

## Rainforest Biome

The largest rainforest in captivity. Find out how rainforests keep us alive and how to help conserve them. Climb to the top on the Rainforest Lookout and maybe win a ticket for a ride in our Canopy Bubble.

Trade and connections: find a smallholding which grows cocoa for chocolate, compare the Malaysian back garden to your own, look out for the huge trading ship. These places are far away but we're connected.

## The Link

(covered Biome entrance)

This grass-roofed building is the entrance to both covered Biomes – it helps keep in the heat. You'll find loos, a shop, membership desks and delicious food. We also do workshops in here and parties from time to time. Busy place!

## Mediterranean Biome

Sights, scents and stories from the Mediterranean, South Africa and California. Water and fertilisers have created global kitchen gardens, but at a cost; explore challenges and solutions, look to the future of the land and its people. Climate change may make conditions even more challenging.

## The Core

Our education, arts and events hub, home to 'the Seed' and our schools programmes. Explore the 'services' that plants provide (climate control, air conditioning, water and waste recycling, carbon capture), the world's largest nutcracker, and how communities can adapt to the needs of the 21st century. Delicious food in Jo's Café too.

## Lift and Bridge

Links Core and Visitor Centre.

## The Visitor Centre

Tickets, annual memberships desks, shop, plant sales, loos. Café and Gallery restaurant (latter also used for functions so check opening times).

## Land train

Every few minutes from top to bottom and bottom to top.

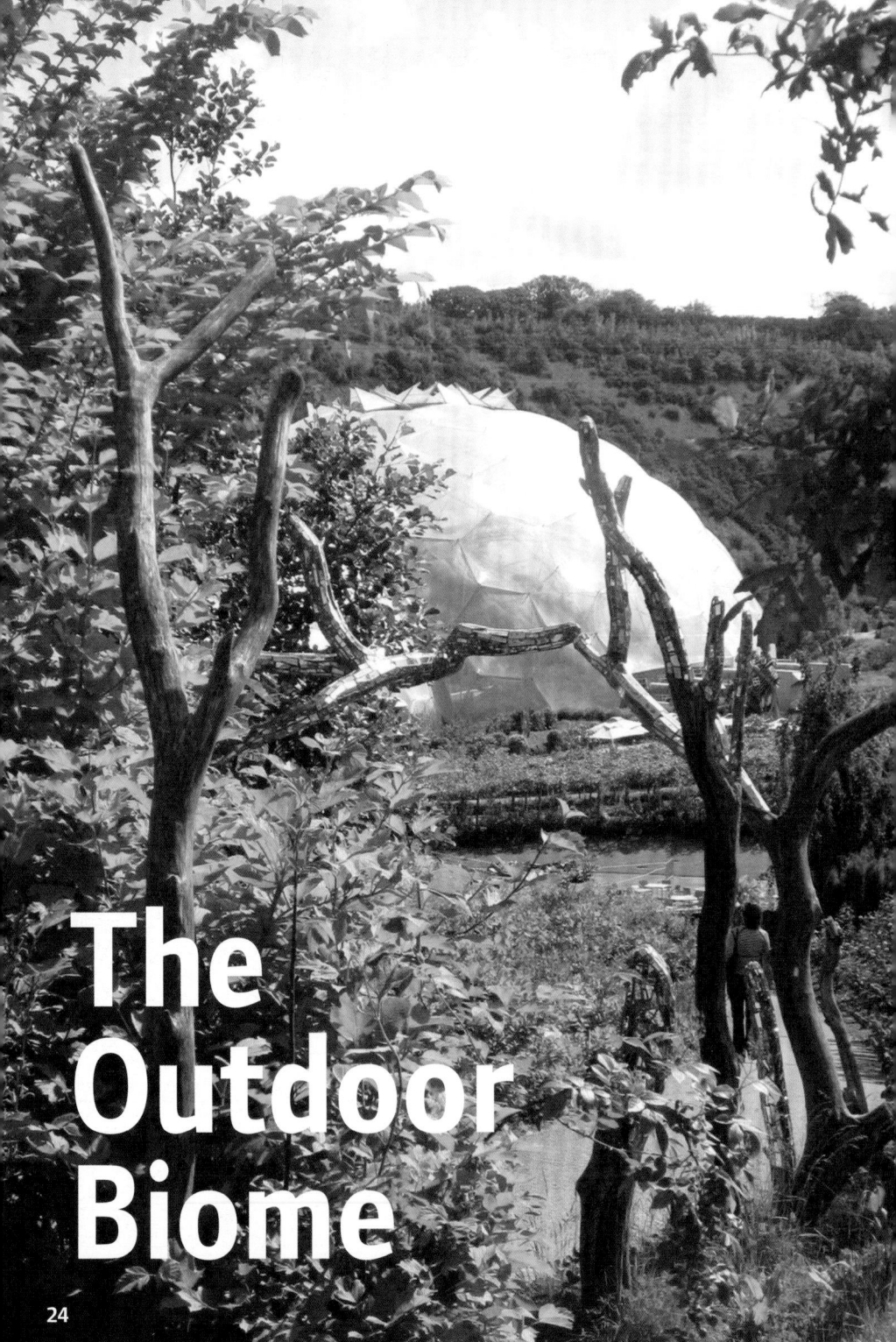

# The
# Outdoor
# Biome

# The Outdoor Biome

### Welcome to the Outdoor Biome  0.01

The viewing platform – outside the Visitor Centre – gives an amazing view over the site. The exhibits below you tell stories of our dependence on the crops that grow in our own climate and show natural environments too. See the map on the inside front cover. The entrance to both covered Biomes is in the grass-covered Link building between them.

## Zigzag area

### Flowerless garden  0.02

Journey through plant evolution, from the earliest mosses to the bryophytes, ferns and horsetails that grew in hot, steamy conditions over 350 million years ago, before the dinosaurs. They created coal as they rotted. Burning it releases the $CO_2$ they locked up and is heating up the planet again. More about climate change in the Core. Also look out for the first flowering plants, Magnolia and Drimys and the Wollemi pine, one of the world's rarest and oldest plants.

### WEEEman  0.03

Our waste giant is made from all the Waste Electrical and Electronic Equipment (about 3.3 tonnes) one person throws away in a lifetime. Designed by Paul Bonomini.

maize

wheat

rice

## Crops that feed the world  0.04

Three plant species – maize, wheat and rice – feed most of the world. They provide carbohydrates and some protein, and store well. Other major staples include potatoes, beans and bananas. Rapid world population growth led to wheat and rice breeding programmes in the 1960s and 70s to increase crop yields. This 'Green Revolution' staved off predicted large-scale starvation.

Today's challenges include a growing population (nearly 7 billion, possibly growing to 10.5 billion by 2050), inequity in distribution, over-consumption and cheap food in many developed countries and hunger in many developing countries, a lack of reserves, rising oil prices, the food/fuel debate (see exhibit 0.18) and climate change. Possible solutions include increasing yields and soil fertility, pest and disease resistance, biotechnology, agricultural biodiversity and new crops that can cope with the changing climate, trade justice, conflict resolution, poverty alleviation, good nutrition projects and education. What can we do? Think about what we eat and where it comes from, waste less, eat less meat (60% of maize production is used as animal feed), grow your own and share food ideas and recipes!

## Garden area

### Flowers and their roots  0.05

For centuries we've brought wild flowers into our gardens and bred our favourites to produce cultivated varieties. Plant hunters also brought plants to our gardens from all over the world. It's not all roses. Some, such as crocosmia, have become invasive.

Cosmos atrosanguineus *(which smells like chocolate) now only exists in cultivation.* Photo: Björn Appel

### The Garden  0.06

There are around 500,000 hectares of gardens in the UK (twice the area of nature reserves). Check out the symbols (the key is on the wooden wall) and pick up some tips.

Gardens give space for play and relaxation, good for the soul and social life.

We use drought-resistant plants rather than bedding plants to save water, such as lavender, rock roses and ornamental grasses. Paths are made of local materials to avoid air miles.

## Plants for taste  0.07

Our chefs use the produce from this garden in the cafés. A productive garden half this size can provide a family with fresh, healthy veg all year round, reducing your carbon footprint and giving a great sense of satisfaction! Feel free to sniff the herbs.

### Seeds, Soup & Sarnies
A Lottery-funded community project engaging people in hands-on grow-your-own courses. **seedssoupsarnies.org**

**People and Gardens** Provides work placements at plant nurseries for people with learning difficulties and people with physical and emotional impairments. They do a great veg-bag scheme. **peopleandgardens.co.uk**

## Stage area

### The Theatre  0.08

Programme details outside the Theatre and on the web.

### Orchard in the making  0.09

Our baby orchard will grow to provide a place of relaxation and fast food (in a biodegradable wrapper). In the UK we only produce around 11% of our own fruit, but interest in health and local produce means orchards are making a comeback. Try growing some tasty old varieties, start a community orchard near you, have an apple day. You can try some Cornish apple juice in our shop.

*I am burns ease.*
*I am wounds nurse.*
*I am ages scent,*
*Heaven sent.*
*I am as purple as veins*
*I am a feeder of flames*
*What am I?*

Annamaria Murphy

### Lavender  0.10

Named from the Latin *lavare* ('to wash'), lavender sedates and soothes. It is used in aromatherapy oils, perfumes, insect repellents and antiseptics.

27

## Pollination  0.11

Plants can't move (much), so they reproduce by luring insects and other animals to take their pollen from flower to flower. Insect/flower relationships are often very specific. Over half our food plants worldwide depend on pollinators, so let's look after them.

## Cornish crops  0.12

Cornwall's climate means it can supply the UK with early crops and quality foods year round. We run a fruit focus group with Tamar Valley Area of Outstanding Natural Beauty to help growers and would-be growers. Community-support agriculture is also on the rise, giving communities access to local, seasonal produce directly from the farmer.

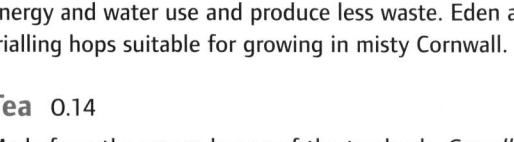

## Beer and brewing  0.13

Look out for beer ingredients (barley and hops), the hop stilt walker, the brewing kettle and the isinglass (tropical catfish swim bladder) used to clear beer, on our hop poles. Environmentally friendly beers are made from new pest- and disease-resistant hops that reduce energy and water use and produce less waste. Eden are trialling hops suitable for growing in misty Cornwall.

## Tea  0.14

Made from the young leaves of the tea bush, *Camellia sinensis*, tea grows in the subtropics, the cool, moist, mountainous tropics – and here! There is renewed interest in its health-giving properties. Many tea-growing areas are already being affected by climate change; in Kenya, Mexico, Peru and Nicaragua growers are taking to higher altitudes at the rate of 3–4m a year.

## Global gardeners  0.15

Sweet potatoes, outdoor chillies and lemongrass, anyone? Discover new veg and fruit to grow in your garden, different ways of growing things and new ways of

eating them, from gardening communities with roots in Africa, Asia, Latin America, the Caribbean and Europe.

The Heritage Seed Library (HSL) conserves rare varieties of vegetables. More info in the little brown shed. Become a HSL member and grow up to six rare varieties each year. **gardenorganic.org.uk/hsl**

Gardens for Life Crossing communities, cultures and countries, Gardens for Life is a network of schools that explores the world through gardening and growing food. Find out more in the blue allotment shed. **edenproject.com/gardens-for-life**

## Eco-engineering  0.16

We use plant roots to stabilize the steep slopes. Extreme gardening in practice!

# New Uses for Crops

Farmers and scientists team up to turn plants into green factories.

## Hemp  0.17

Industrial hemp provides food and health products, clothing, car components and building materials. Hempcrete (hemp and lime) has a much lower carbon footprint than concrete as a walling material. Hemp grows well in the UK, needing few agro-chemical inputs (whereas cotton uses around 25% of the world's pesticides). Legally we have to have a barrier round our hemp crop, so George Fairhurst designed us a hemp fence.

## Food, fuel or plastic?  0.18

Sunflowers and oil seed rape (OSR) are bred to provide high-quality oils for lubrication, plastic manufacture and biodiesel as well as food. Plant sugars and starch from maize and wheat make bioethanol for fuel and compostable plastic cutlery, carrier bags, nappies, etc. The UK's first bioethanol plant opened in 2010, creating a new market for wheat and mopping up the surplus we usually export. Plants grown for biofuels are having their carbon footprint scrutinised and the food-versus-fuel debate means a search for alternative raw materials. Biomass to Liquids (BTL) factories are being developed to turn waste straw, wood waste, stalks, etc, into fuel, even biokerosene to power aircraft.

One football pitch (0.9 hectare) of oil seed rape could make enough biofuel to power your car for a year (10 to 15 thousand miles).
One football pitch (0.9 hectare) of maize can produce 400,000 plastic drinking cups.

## Fibres and new materials  O.19

Strong plant fibres can be made into rope, cloth and bio-composites (plant fibres in resin). Growing here are some of the tough guys: flax, nettle, New Zealand flax and agave (sisal). Nettles can be made into sofa fabric, hemp and flax (embedded in resin) into car panels, and we've even found a fishing rod made of carrot fibre. Tug George Fairhurst's metal giant to see how strong plant fibres are.

## West Side

### Prairie  O.20

Looks great in full flower in August. The American prairies were partially created by man, using controlled burning to attract game (to young post-fire grass) and ease travelling. They once covered a quarter of the US. In some areas, up to 99% have been destroyed in the last 150 years. Work is underway to conserve these diverse grasslands and let the buffalo roam once more. Why conserve? Provision of ecosystem services (see Core exhibits), climate control and potential future crops for starters. We manage our prairie by burning in Feb/March, then the plants start to come through: *Camassias, Liatris, Echinaceas* ...

*Echinacea*

Some public parks are now turning to prairie-style plantings: better for biodiversity, cheaper and easier to maintain than bedding.

### Plants for a changing climate  O.21

Our Green Team of extreme gardeners explore adaptation and try new plants in tricky situations. Our Echiums (big blue flower spikes) loved the hot, dry summer but got clobbered in winter 2010. Onwards and upwards!

## Biomass fuels 0.22

David Kemp's 'Industrial Plant' sculpture and his 'Greenhouse of New Worlds' take a sideways look at fossil fuels, which currently provide around 85% of the world's energy. The developed world (16% of the world's population) uses 53% of this energy, while nearly half the world's people (mainly in developing countries) rely on wood, charcoal and dung which have a low carbon footprint: the amount of $CO_2$ absorbed during their growth equals the amount emitted on burning. Willow, poplar and miscanthus are burnt for biomass in the UK. Other energy choices include wind and water power, algae as fuel, solar and nuclear power and geothermal, using heat from the earth: we've now got planning permission to install our own geothermal energy plant.

## Myth and folklore 0.23

Stories keep plants alive in our memory, and our Pollinators bring you tales across the site. Pete Hill and Kate Munro created our willow Dream Chamber.

Its classic seven-ring labyrinth is found worldwide. To sailors it was a good-luck token, ensuring safe return. It provided protection against wandering spirits who get lost in the curves (spirits can only travel in straight lines, allegedly). In medieval times it stood for a model of the cosmos with seven heavenly bodies circling the earth. It has also been a focus for meditation. Mazes aim to confuse; the labyrinth is a journey, and perhaps the path takes you in a direction you are not expecting.

## Wild Cornwall 0.24

Cornwall's biodiversity, its varied landscapes, habitats and wildlife, have been shaped by its climate, geology, geography and people. Heathlands are partly man-made; they started forming 6,000 to 3,500 years ago when woodland was cleared for hunting and agriculture, and need managing to

Early gentian
*Gentianella anglica*

31

prevent them reverting. Since 1800 Cornwall has lost over 90% of its lowland heath. Conservationists in Cornwall are helping restore, protect and manage what is left. In Cornwall 75% of the land is farmed, though farming also provides rich habitats. Sculptors Peter Martin and Sarah Stewart-Smith have immortalised rare Cornish species in stone. Chris Drury created the Cloud Chamber. We planted 45 species in the area, plus a few seeds from wild plants around the site – now there are 160 species. How many can you find?

## Natural England Juniper Conservation

Conservation of the threatened dwarf Juniper (*Juniperus communis* subsp. *hemisphaerica*), which grows in a small population on the Lizard in Cornwall. Our Green Team is propagating it to help safeguard it.

*Eve, Myth and Folklore (p.31)*

## Mining the earth: metals, minerals and energy

*Core copper roof (p.34)*

We're just as dependent on mining as we are on agriculture. But the environmental and social impact can be serious, both in the short and long term, and it is crucial to understand the industry's role and what constitutes good practice and responsible mining. The Eden Project, created in a 170-year-old china-clay quarry, is a world-class example of the reclamation of an old mineral site. Eden has formed the Post Mining Alliance to work with industry and grassroots community groups to encourage and promote the regeneration of old mines so as to bring maximum benefit to the local community and the environment. **postmining.org**

# Core Side

## Health 0.26

Half the herbs sold worldwide are wild-harvested, which, when done responsibly, can sustain environments and livelihoods. Herbs and pharmaceuticals (e.g. morphine derived from opium poppies) are also grown as crops. With 'pharming', crops are modified and used as biological factories to produce drugs.

## Dyes 0.27

Woad and indigo give us blue, weld yellow and madder red. Indigo-dyed cloth comes out of the dye vat yellow and turns blue as it oxidises in the air.

## Paper 0.28

Plants growing here can be made into paper. Many natural habitats have been cleared and planted with *Eucalyptus* and *Pinus radiata* for paper-making. Agricultural residues containing cellulose, such as wheat and rice straw, can be used instead of wood pulp. World paper consumption is rocketing – so is recycling, luckily.

## The Spiral Garden 0.29

Making a school or community garden? Discover some low-cost ideas: willow spirals, rainbows of flowers, soft paths, textured plants, spooky plants and scented plants.

## Timber 0.30

The plant labels are made from the timber they describe. Wood is a carbon store and timber construction is on the rise. Good for wood.

# Outer Estate

**Forest Garden** On your way out from the Visitor Centre, explore our new Forest Garden – full of native plants for food, shelter and medicines.

**Wild Chile** Behind Pineapple car park take a trip to Chile and explore our forest of beautiful plants. This 'Safe Site' contains and protects wild-collected material from the Valdivian forests of central Chile – a living example of ex-situ conservation. We are working with the Royal Botanic Garden, Edinburgh, and the International Conifer Conservation Programme.

Why? Central Chile is under threat from logging, agriculture and replacement with non-native pine and eucalyptus for paper and wood chip. Damaged environments *can* be repaired with effective stewardship.

# The Core

## Eden's education, arts and events hub

The Core isn't just a building, it's a metaphor. Its structure is based on a sunflower, which isn't a single flower but a collaborative project between hundreds of flowers which have united to create something better. Our projects, many of which are described in the Core, show how much can be achieved by working together.

The Seed, a 75-tonne sculpture carved from Cornish granite by Peter Randall Page, brings nature's blueprint into the heart of the building and plants a symbol of hope, to grow ideas for the 21st century. You can get up close on the ground floor.

# How the Core was built

**The brief** Fit for purpose, future-proof, made with responsibly sourced materials, energy efficient, with minimal waste. Grimshaws played another blinder, helped immeasurably by funding from the Millennium Commission, the South West Regional Development Agency and Cornwall's Objective One Programme.

## The structure
Double-curved glulam (glued laminated) timber beams, Swiss Forestry Stewardship Council endorsed.

## The form
Inspired by the growth blueprint of plants, opposing spirals based on Fibonacci's sequence: 0, 1, 1, 2, 3, 5, 8, 13, 21, 34 ... where every number is the sum of the previous two. The spirals on a pinecone, pineapple and sunflower, like our roof, usually represent two consecutive numbers in this sequence.

## The roof
40% of the world's copper is recycled. What about the other 60%, we wondered? Because of the way the market operates it can be almost impossible for the end user to ensure that metals are responsibly produced and sourced.

We traced the supply chain of the copper for our roof from a single Rio Tinto mine, known for its high environmental and social standards, all the way to Eden. This unusual initiative has led to much more work on the minerals supply chain.

## Accessibility
The Core is on three floors, and built into the landscape so that each one is accessible from ground level.

## Floors
You'll find recycled wood, plant-based floorings (Marmoleum from flax, carpets from maize), and concrete from china-clay sand (low carbon footprint). The little green tiles are made from recycled Heineken bottles.

## What's inside the Core?

### Ground floor

The huge glass ball of the Plant Engine represents the world's ecosystems (rainforests, oceans, grasslands, etc). It breathes life into the bell jars containing automata representing the 'ecosystem services' that keep us alive: controlling our climate, cleaning our air, recycling our water and waste, capturing our carbon and providing inspiration. Have a look at the cartoons round the bell jars to discover some of the amazing things the planet does for us – all for free – if we look after it.

Three challenges we impose on these systems – climate change, clean water provision, biodiversity loss – are explored in the little greenhouse, water tank and curiosity cabinet.

### Biodiversity

Life in all its richness and variety. Nature is important, we're part of it and it keeps us alive. Human impact is causing many species to disappear, and with them the patterns of life and the outputs that our lives, economies and societies depend on. Biodiversity loss is an issue, because if it goes too far we will be among its first victims.

### First floor

This is where the classrooms for our schools programmes are (not open to the public, sorry). You'll also find temporary exhibitions and films here.

### Second floor

Susan Derges created the windows around the solar terrace on this floor to symbolise the water cycle. On this floor you will also find delicious food in Jo's Café.

# The Rainforest Biome

# Your tour guide to the Rainforest Biome

> 'Rainforest is the glue that holds the climate of our planet together. Lose the forest and it will have devastating consequences for all life on Earth.'
>
> **Professor Sir Ghillean Prance, FRS**

### Welcome to the Rainforest Biome R.01

The Humid Tropic Regions are located between the Tropics of Cancer and Capricorn, approximately 23.5° N and S of the Equator. The average temperature is 25°C all year round (5°C variation), with over 90% humidity and 1,500 mm (60") annual rainfall.

## Rainforests are the planet's life-support system

They control the earth's climate. They absorb and store $CO_2$ in their wood. They make huge white clouds, which reflect heat, keeping the earth cool, and help maintain rain cycles that water crops across the world.

Millions of people live in and make their living from the rainforests. Many products we use every day originated there: chocolate, coffee, spices, rubber, medicines – and you'll find plenty more right here in the Biome.

Rainforests cover 5% of the earth and are home to half the world's plant and animal species. Every week new species are discovered – 1,200 in the last decade.

## What's the problem?

Forests are cleared for agriculture, mining, development and timber. An area of primary forest the size of Eden's Rainforest Biome is destroyed every 10 seconds.

Climate change 12–20% of carbon emissions come from deforestation. To win the battle against climate change we need to stop cutting rainforests down as well as reduce our $CO_2$ levels.

Biodiversity loss Over 100 species may be lost every day in the rainforests. Orangutans' homes are destroyed when forests are felled to grow oil palm, found in nearly half the bestselling products in supermarkets.

## What is being done?

Rainforests can re-grow or be replanted and managed sustainably for the future. We need to help the forests to survive to ensure our future survival.

Reducing Emissions from Deforestation and Forest Degradation (REDD) encourages developing countries to protect/manage their forests by creating a financial value for the carbon stored in the trees (making them worth more standing than logged). REDD+ goes further, to include conservation, sustainable management and enhancement, and encourages further investment in low-carbon development – and a healthier, greener tomorrow.

The United Nations has declared 2011 the International Year of Forests.

## What can we do?

Understand how the forests keep us alive, and explore ways of keeping them alive.

Support charities and organisations working to save the forest.

Shop for products which look after the forest (eg. FSC, Rainforest Alliance) and avoid products that don't (not just oil palm; forests are often felled to grow soya and meat).

Write letters on rainforest issues to politicians at home and abroad.

Volunteer for a rainforest charity (here or there).

---

### Protecting fragile forests

Forest Restoration Research Unit (FORRU) – NW Thailand, works with communities to regenerate rainforests. **forru.org**

Eden is helping to conserve the Atlantic subtropical rainforests of Argentina, by developing a sustainable management plan for the Yabotí

Biosphere Reserve. Logging and agriculture has left only 5% of this 'biodiversity hotspot' standing, which is also critical for the survival of the local Guaraní people.

*IKOS pod*

*Canopy Bubble*

## The Rainforest Lookout and Canopy Bubble

The jungle canopy is the last high frontier, usually only seen by intrepid explorers. Every day scientists discover more about the canopy: the biodiversity it holds, how the rainforest cleans our atmosphere, how the rainforest controls our climate, how essential the rainforest is for all life on earth. Now you can see what they see, and get an amazing bird's eye view of the whole Biome from 50 metres above the ground on our new Rainforest Lookout (p.38). The Canopy Bubble is the real McCoy, used by canopy scientists. Our crew use it to prune and check for pests, and for events, though visitors can sometimes win rides. You'll also spot our IKOS pod: mobile living quarters that usually sits high in the trees, though at Eden it sits on the ground so that everyone can see it. We're in the throes of fundraising to build a canopy walkway and a series of interactive rainforest adventures to make the experience even more real.

## Explore the world's rainforests

The *Tropic Trader*: your gateway to the rainforests of the tropical islands, Malaysia, West Africa and tropical South America. Different regions have different plant species but their shapes are similar, having evolved to cope with the hot, steamy conditions (huge leaves, drip tips for shedding water). Discover stories from the peoples who live in these forests, the challenges, their advice. Further round, cross into the crops and cultivation zone, and see how many plants from the forest you use regularly.

## Tropical islands: conserving the land  R.02

Mangrove swamps protect the coast (e.g. against tsunamis), provide fuel, timber and a habitat for fish. Island habitats are home to many unusual, unique species. Climate change, invasive species, human settlement and tourism pose serious threats. Isolated island communities lack resources to conserve biodiversity, though conservation programmes offer hope: the rare Seychelles Coco-de-Mer, with huge seeds that look like giant bottoms, was over-harvested (as trophies and perceived aphrodisiacs). Now each seed is registered and protected. Ours (a gift from the Seychelles) germinated five years after planting: one of very few specimens in the UK, it grows slowly – a leaf a year. *Impatiens gordonii* (Seychelles) is threatened by loss of habitat. Eden, conservation bodies in the Seychelles and Reading University are propagating and conserving it.

Coco-de-Mer seeds

Impatiens gordonii

The Maldives  These Indian Ocean islands make up one of the lowest-lying countries in the world – more than 80% less than 1 metre above sea level. With leadership from President Nasheed, they are working to become carbon neutral within 10 years. Eden is working with them on a range of initiatives.

## Malaysia: Orang dan Kebun (people and garden)  R.03

The contemporary Malaysian home garden provides food year-round. Herbs and flowers nearest the house, vegetables, fruit, and other useful trees further out. Winged beans replace our runner beans; both fertilise the soil. Pak choi, taro and rice replace cabbage, carrots and potatoes.

The garden also provides building materials, medicines and produce to barter or sell at local markets. The miracle tree, *Moringa oleifera*, has edible leaves, beans, flowers and roots. Its seeds are used as water filters and its oils for watchmaking. To the left of the path is a rice paddy. In Asia 'rice is life', culturally and spiritually crucial to people's lives.

## West Africa: managing the land R.04

The totems, by West African sculptor El Anatsui, came from charred timbers recycled from a part of Falmouth docks which was destroyed by fire. They started their life as trees in West Africa.

On your right, penjaw: high forest is partially cleared and selected trees left to provide fruits, spices and medicines. Further round, the chop farm, where areas of forest are cleared, grows light-loving crops such as groundnuts, cassava and traditional African leafy vegetables alongside pawpaw, baobab and mango. Reverting to traditional crops in these areas rather than high-status Western crops helps provide a balanced diet and an income from local markets.

Our bantaba meeting place was created with help from the Ballabu Conservation Project, which hopes to create sustainable projects in and around 14 Gambian villages. We've a Gardens for Life project there too.

## Tropical South America:
## shamanic art, cassava and forest gardening R.05

Take the steep and stepped high road past the waterfall for a great panoramic view and see the work of Peruvian shamanic artists Montes Shuna and Panduro Baneo, showing a spiritual connection between plants and people.

The flat low road takes you past the tallest tree in the Biome (the kapok). The paths meet at the tropical forest garden which grows useful plants – for food, fuel, medicines and materials – as a natural forest system. Near the clearing a hut shows the processing of cassava into tapioca. Cassava varieties contain prussic acid (hydrocyanide), which has to be removed before cooking!

## Crops and cultivation
R.06

Here you will find the products we use every day – soya, cola, rubber, cocoa, chocolate, bananas … Will Jackson and Paul Spooner made us the arch where products meet their makers.

## Soya R.07

Soya crops up in around 70% of our supermarket products. Full of protein, low in saturated fats and cholesterol free, it is also a meat- and dairy-free alternative. But with an area 3.5 times the size of the UK being grown every year, much on land that was previously rainforest, the impact is huge. Demand for soya for oil, cattle fodder and biofuels is still growing. The Roundtable on Sustainable Soy (**responsiblesoy.org**) promotes sustainable production, processing and trading. We can help by choosing sustainably grown soya products.

## Gum and cola R.08

Cola, an African tree with caffeine-rich seeds, was once found in cola drinks, and the milky latex from the sapodilla tree, *Manilkara zapota*, made gum. Today alternative plants and synthetics are used.

## Rubber R.09

South American rubber trees, *Hevea brasiliensis*, provided rubber for boots and balls for centuries. In the 1700s Europeans stepped in with waterproof clothing and catheters. Spiralling demand for car tyres stimulated the cultivated rubber industry in Asia. Synthetic rubber, from oil, came in when wars restricted supply. Rising oil prices and AIDs-related demand for condoms and rubber gloves let natural rubber bounce back. Real rubber is also needed for high-spec uses such as aircraft tyres. Today, some rubber is sourced from designated areas of rainforest rather than plantations. We're now tapping the milky latex from our rubber trees right here.

## Re-growing the forest  R.10

6 million hectares of primary forest are lost or modified every year – the area of our Rainforest Biome every 10 seconds. Replanting pioneer trees quickly creates canopy cover, suppresses weeds, attracts animals that bring in seeds and nurtures timber tree species. Eden works on projects that help (p.40).

## Cocoa and chocolate  R.11

Cocoa originated in South America – you'll find its history on the cocoa wall. Today it is grown by around 2.5 million farmers, mainly on West African smallholdings. The UK chocolate industry supports schemes such as Fairtrade, improving livelihoods and protecting locals from global price fluctuations. Fairtrade also gives a premium that can be reinvested in business, social and environmental schemes. Scientists are crossing West African cocoa trees with their wild South American ancestors (we've some growing on the bottom path) to create

*Ghanaian cocoa farmers from the Kuapa Kokoo Co-operative admiring Eden's cocoa crop*

disease-resistant trees – fewer chemicals and less planting on new land.

## Palms  R.12

Palms are used for walls, thatch, ropes, boats, sago, sugar and cooking oil. The hut here has a palm-leaf roof. It was built by  Penan tribespeople  from Sarawak  who came to Eden to  raise awareness of the impact  oil palm plantations are having on their ancestral land. **bmf.ch/en** Palm oil is found in many processed foods, cleaning products and cosmetics. Supply chases demand and plantations march into the rainforest. In 2002 the Roundtable on Sustainable Palm Oil (RSPO) was established to address concerns. It is currently trialling a certification system. **sustainable-palmoil.org** We no longer use palm oil in our Cornish pasties.

## Coffee  R.13

Often under 10% of the retail price of this valuable product is earned by the exporting countries. Beans ripen at different times, so labour is intensive; mechanisation increases productivity but reduces quality. Our sustainably grown Eden-brand coffee uses Rainforest Alliance-certified beans, shade-grown under diverse trees, preserving biodiversity and helping mitigate the expected effects of climate change (higher temperatures, drought).

## Sugar R.14

Sugar is made from tropical sugar cane (and temperate sugar beet). In the 1300s we each used around a teaspoon a year. Today it's 35 kg, and stories of diabetes, obesity and poor teeth abound.

Sugar cane is also used for ethanol production. It doesn't get caught in the food or fuel debate (like maize) and doesn't displace rainforest, according to the industry. Bagasse, the waste product, can be burnt to generate electricity. Seven million people are employed worldwide in the sugar industry, many in developing countries. Fairtrade and organic sugar are also on the up; all our sugar is Fairtrade.

## Mangoes R.15

For us a delicious treat (and a promising export crop for developing countries), for others a vital famine food. The flesh makes medicines and wine; the nut oil cosmetics; and the wood, traditional drums and furniture.

## Bananas R.16

Over 85% of the bananas grown in the tropics stay there, a staple diet for millions. Different varieties provide savoury or sweet dishes, juice, wine and beer. The banana conveyor and second hut tell the story of the bananas that reach our shores: the Cavendish types from large plantations (such as those in Latin America, usually owned by large companies) or from

smallholdings (such as those in the Caribbean, usually owned by local farmers). Organic and/or fairly traded crops appeal to concerned consumers – look at the label to make your choice. Panama disease has blighted Cavendish crops worldwide, so growers are trying new varieties – and so are we.

## Tropical fruits R.17

When it's available we put tangy lulo in our smoothies. Colombian local charities and the government are helping farmers grow and market these fruits. This could help provide an alternative cash crop to coca (*Erythroxylum coca*) – used to make cocaine. We also sometimes serve baobab ice cream and baobab jam in our sponges. Baobab, which tastes a bit like sherbet, helps support some growers in Africa.

## Bamboo R.18

Used by half the world's people to make homes, furniture, food, fuel, music, medicine, scaffolding and suspension bridges, bamboo's hollow tubes are strong but light. Within its tissues short, tough fibres sit in a resilient matrix: nature's fibreglass. Housings and Hazards, who bring people together to develop affordable, low-impact housing for vulnerable rural communities, helped make our house – Bam-Bams. Come in, sit and relax, maybe a game of chess?

## Tropical biofuels R.19

In the tropics they're looking at *Jatropha*, oil palm, soya and sugar cane to make bioethanol and biodiesel. There are pros and cons.

## Pineapples R.20

Pineapples tend to be produced on huge farms with high levels of fertilisers and pesticides, though organic techniques and GM technology are being explored to reduce inputs. Fairtrade pineapples are on the increase too.

## Spices R.21

Today spices are cheap. In the past they were worth their weight in gold and shaped the world as we know it. Though nutmeg was thought to cure the bubonic plague, it was along the spice route from Central Asia that the Black Death first travelled to Europe in the mid-1300s.

## Cashews R.22

Why are cashews so expensive? Roasting, shelling and cleaning the nuts is laborious and the shells contain highly corrosive cashew-nut shell liquor (CNSL). Traditionally used to treat ringworm, CNSL is now sometimes used in heatproof enamels and brake pads.

## Life in the treetops R.23

We've brought the gardens that usually exist high in the canopy down to meet you: orchids, Dutchman's pipes. You may occasionally spot a tree frog in the watery pools of the bromeliads.

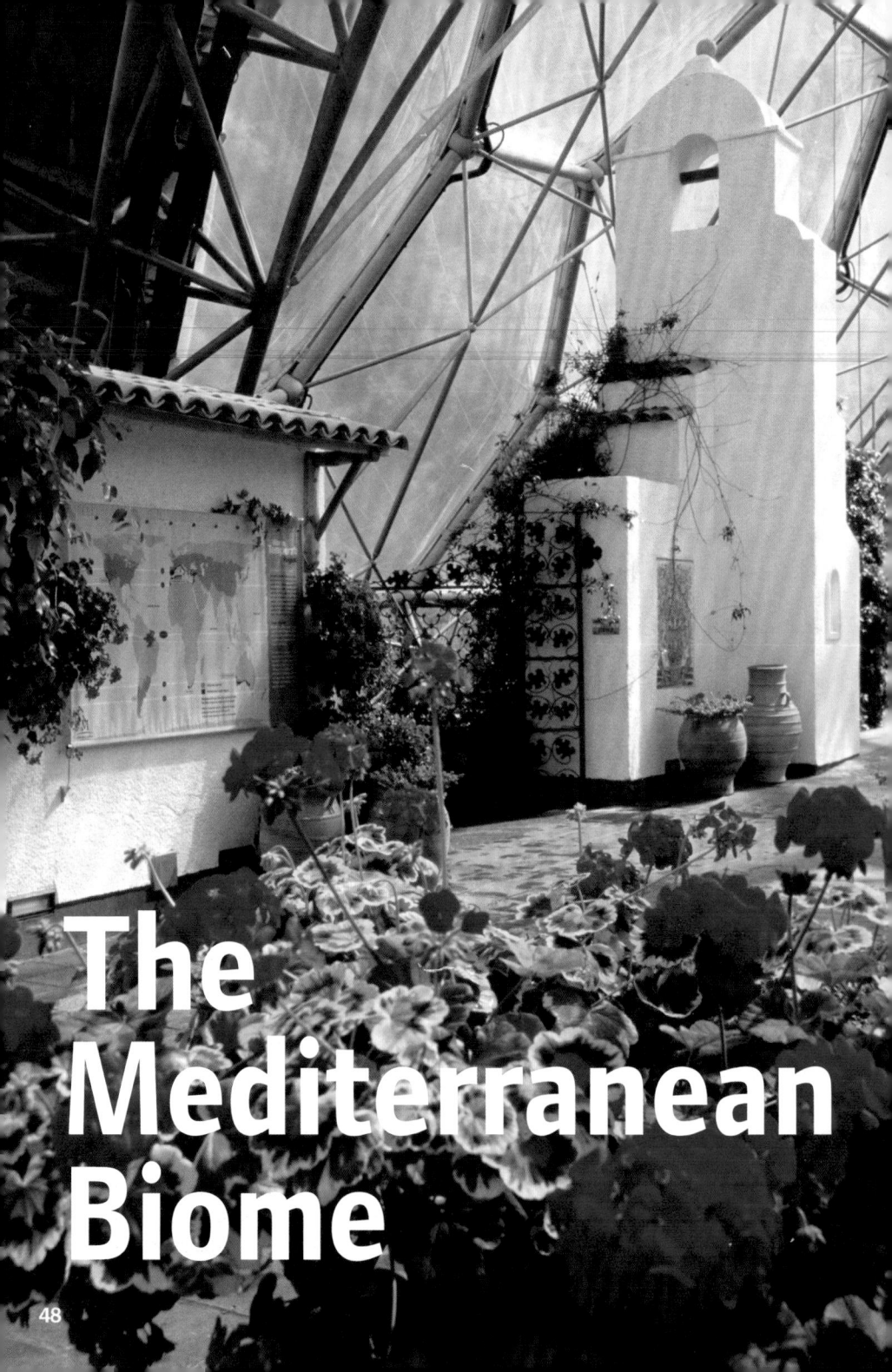

# The Mediterranean Biome

# Your tour guide to the Mediterranean Biome

Salutare! Enter all — The Lands of the Warm Temperate Regions
Discover:
The Mediterranean's Paradise
California's Horn of Plenty
South Africa's Garden
History and Olives
Oranges and Dust
Fertile Deserts
Culture's Cradle
Born of Sister Fire and Brother Drought

## Welcome to the Mediterranean Biome  M.01

Mediterranean-type climates (part of the
Warm Temperate climate zone), with their
strong sun, hot, dry summers and cool, wet
winters, are located 30–40°N or S latitude on
the western sides of continents. In this Biome
you will find stories from the Mediterranean,
South Africa and California. We may enjoy
these climates, but the native plants cope with
drought and poor, thin soils. Some have small,
grey, hairy leaves, some make protective oils,
some are spiny, evergreen and/or waxy. This
may help to reduce water loss and make the
plants less appetising to predators. The plants

are tough but their environments are fragile: intensive grazing erodes soils, imported
plants threaten native species and land is developed – big pressure on small lands.
Water and fertilisers have created massive kitchen gardens for vegetables, wines, fruit
and flowers. Explore the impacts, challenges, effects
of climate change and some possible solutions.

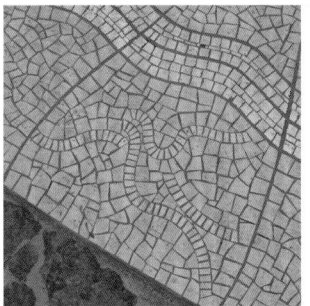

## The Mediterranean Basin  M.02

Through the gates to your left, visit a typical
Mediterranean garden. Back on the main, lower route
(no steps), the 'Liquid Gold' mosaic path created by
Elaine Goodwin celebrates the tradition of olive oil as
a symbol of life and divinity. Look for the subtle dove
images – one for each Mediterranean nation.

49

The Mediterranean landscape is mainly man-made, cleared for crops over many thousands of years, including the olives and vines that helped shape this region's civilisation. The ancient terraced olive groves support more animal species than a pine forest. Today many people leave their mountain farms seeking work on the coast, although city dwellers are beginning to return to smallholdings. Buying traditional foods and natural products, seeking out quality and taste, farm holidays: all can help conserve these fragile environments and communities.

Past the bell tower, the upper stepped route takes you through Maquis and Garrigue to the viewing point. The French underground movement in World War II was called the Maquis because they hid in this hilly landscape of prickly oak, juniper and broom, a habitat that contains unique plants, insects and reptiles, but can get overlooked, having no spectacular birds or mammals.

### South Africa  M.03

The Cape Floral Kingdom has over 1,400 plant species which are rare or endangered. Fynbos, with around 7,000 species (5,000 unique to this area), covers 80% of this kingdom. 'Fain-boss', Afrikaans for 'fine bush', refers to the evergreen, fire-prone shrubs in this nutrient-poor soil. Plants include rush-like restioids, shrubby heathers and proteoids, with their stunning feather-like blooms. Formed millions of years ago from the ashes of drought-stressed forests, the Fynbos has been fire-managed for conservation since the 1960s. Protea seeds need exposure to smoke to germinate. The Fynbos is threatened by agricultural and urban development, uncontrolled fire and invasive alien tree species.

Little Karoo   In this semi-arid valley behind the southern coastal mountain range, the land bakes to 50°C in summer, freezes in winter and suffers severe droughts. Today much of the valley is irrigated for crops, but the surrounding hills house ice plants, aloes and types of daisy.

Namaqualand   This red desert, 250 miles north of Cape Town, blooms into a multi-coloured carpet after winter rain. Different species germinate in different years, depending on when the rains come, taking it in turns to share the scarce water. Descendants of these wild plants, pelargoniums and daisies, are garden favourites.

## Green Futures College, South Africa

Students are enrolled from townships, locally and from the Eastern Cape, where there is much unemployment, to study conservation, horticulture and eco-tourism guiding courses. This helps conserve the local plants and habitats, raises awareness of issues, develops life skills and provides employment. Our staff work there and we host their students here. **greenfutures.co.za**

## California  M.04

California has vast landscapes and a huge diversity of plants. Ceanothus and Californian poppies, familiar garden plants, grow wild here. The spiky chaparral, with its less familiar buck bush, toyon and scrub oak (the 'chaparro'), gave its name to chaparreros, or 'chaps', worn by cowboys to protect their legs. Chaparral, grassland and the open oak forests were the results of thousands of years of controlled burning by Native Americans.

California once had such a rich natural harvest that the indigenous people had no need to develop agriculture. Today water is so valuable that environmental activists take out court orders to make farmers leave minimum flows in rivers. The state's high consumption brings social and environmental costs, putting it at the forefront of climate change. On the other hand, the region is also the birthplace of innovative new technology and home to some of today's most environmentally conscious people. The catalytic converter started life here and 2010 saw the first legislation to give polluting companies such as utilities and refineries financial incentives to emit fewer greenhouse gases.

## Crops and cultivation  M.05

Many of the crops in our exhibits section are seasonal, so change from time to time. Producing vegetables, fruits and flowers in the world's Mediterranean regions is an intensive industry using fertiliser, water, sprays and often immigrant labour. Pressure is mounting to move to low-input, energy-efficient, diversified farming. Water is becoming increasingly scarce; aquifers of the Campo de Nijar region in Almeria (Spain) have more than twice the volume of water extracted from them every year than they receive. Technologies are being developed to reduce usage and explore the re-use of clean seawater or waste water. Look out for ideas around the Biome, for example Autopots **autopot.co.uk** and the Seawater Greenhouse **seawatergreenhouse.com**.

## Cork  M.06

Cork oak wood pastures are rich in plant and animal biodiversity and show agriculture and conservation working hand in hand. Cork is harvested from the tree's bark and high-value ham is obtained from the Iberian pigs (represented here by Heather Jansch's cork pig sculptures) that feed on the acorns. The pigs also help to maintain the diversity of the other plants. Cork trees, unlike other trees, don't die when their bark is cut off, it actually re-grows, so buying cork products supports cork oak wood pastures. Currently supply is outstripping demand (many wines, for example, now use screw tops), the young are moving away from the farms in Portugal, and climate change is also taking its

toll with for example, desertification issues in African cork producing areas. The WWF works to protect these fragile habitats and promotes industries that benefit local rural communities. The Portuguese Cork Association, APCOR, campaigns to promote cork worldwide. Buying wine (and champagne!) with real corks helps. Cork has many other uses too, such as gaskets in engines – it can cope in extreme temperatures. Could new industrial uses help save these landscapes?

## Fruits, nuts, veg and waterwise growing  M.07

The classic Mediterranean diet of fresh veg, fruit, olive oil and a drop of red wine is associated with health and long life. Grow your own Med. veg with our Italian seeds, available in the shop. Peaches, nectarines, loquats, apricots and kiwis from China and almonds from Central to Western Asia have moved to the Mediterranean and California to soak up the sun and the water from the irrigation lines.

## Citrus  M.08

The citrus family is fond of breeding. Clementines are a cross between mandarins and bitter Seville oranges, and tangelos the offspring of tangerines and grapefruits. Citrus fruits provide Vitamin C and nutraceuticals (more on

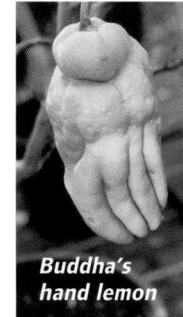

*Buddha's hand lemon*

these in the Core café). Citrus oils are used in flavourings, cleaning products, perfume, anti-bacterial agents, CFC substitutes and even fuel.

## Grape vines M.09

Tim Shaw created this wild Bacchanal where dancing Maenads mirroring the shapes of the vines surround their god, depicted here as a bull. Bacchus (aka Dionysus) started out with good intentions as the god of vegetation. Things changed when he went from growing the vine to drinking its fermented juices – party time! Dionysus stands straddled between the ancient cultivated landscapes of the Mediterranean and the irrigated lands of today's intensive agriculture. Some of the classic wine grapes seen here go back to the days when Bacchus was revered. As our climate changes vineyards are beginning to spread northwards – Cornish wines are highly regarded.

## Cut flowers/cotton M.10

Cut flowers 85% of our cut flowers are imported from the Netherlands, Colombia, Israel, Ecuador, Spain, Italy, Ethiopia, Kenya and elsewhere. This causes many environmental and social challenges but there's also potential for jobs and a step out of poverty. Check out the label. Seasonal blooms with low 'flower miles' mean you can say it with sustainable flowers! **edenproject.com/shop**

Cotton Used for clothing but also found in toothpaste, nappies, explosives, cosmetics, bank notes, ice cream, cattle feed and photographic film. It is the world's biggest non-food crop, makes over a third of the world's textiles and traditionally uses high levels of water, fertiliser and pesticides. Organic and fairly traded cotton are on the increase: look at the label, your wallet is your weapon! Visit our New Uses for Crops exhibit in the Outdoor Biome (O.19) to see other plant fibres entering the market.

## Chillies and peppers/Winter displays M.11

There are dozens of chilli varieties, ranging in heat from mild to unbearable. Chilli heat is measured in Scoville Heat Units, and the hottest variety found so far is rated at 1,382,118 SHU, whereas your basic supermarket green chilli comes in at 1,500! Chillies and sweet peppers are easy to grow – you'll find seeds in the Eden shop.

## Seasonal crops M.12

Tobacco Brought to Europe by Columbus and heralded as a miracle medicine centuries before its link to cancer. Besides its health risks the crop also depletes soil fertility and requires much spraying. However it also provides livelihoods for some growers in developing countries. What to do? Create support mechanisms to help the growers find alternative crops or find an alternative use for tobacco? Scientists are currently exploring 'pharming' tobacco, modifying it to produce a vaccine for non-Hodgkin's lymphoma and to make antibodies that act as HIV-neutralising agents.

Small grains They feed millions who live on the dry edges of the world and also provide local employment and income generation via production of nutritious snacks for more affluent urban areas. The grains have great potential in light of climate change and water shortages.

Sunflowers and globe artichokes Both are types of daisy.

## Olives M.13

Once olive oil provided light for lamps and anointed the brave. Now used mostly in the kitchen, it is thought to reduce cholesterol levels and deter heart disease. Production is up but the squeeze is on to reduce chemical inputs. Our older olive trees came from Sicily, having reached the end of their productive life. Debbie Prosser made the olive oil vats. There is as much variation in taste and character in olive oil as there is in wine.

medicine chest ... heart's rest ... blood cleaner ... hair redeemer ... lover's liquid ... skin smoother ... fever calm ... mother's balm ... super food...

## A taste of the Mediterranean

In November 2010 Eden had a flood and we lost most of our kitchens and cafés in the Link (although by the time you read this it should all be rebuilt). While we mopped up we decided to do what we've been thinking about for ages – serve food in the Biome. So from time to time you'll find us trying out pizzas, lamb kebabs, risottos and lots of other Mediterranean goodies.

'A smell can be overwhelmingly nostalgic because it triggers powerful images and emotions before we have time to edit them.'

Diane Ackerman
*A Natural History of the Senses*

## Perfume   M.14

Feel free to touch and sniff. Try to describe the scent without referring to another smell. Tricky, isn't it? The scent of violets, a whiff of mint – scent goes straight to the seat of emotion and memory in the ancestral core of your brain. Plants use scent to attract pollinators and repel predators.

Do we use it to signal, seduce or warn, like plants, or for sweet memory and comfort? We can detect over 10,000 different odours, and perfumiers use this to full effect, making scents from a range of plant extracts just as musicians use notes to compose melodies.

# What can we all do?

There's no shortage of top tips for a greener life: fitting energy-saving light-bulbs and so on. Useful? Yes and no.

They can trivialise the issues; saving the world isn't a matter of what goes in your basket, and it takes the heat off the big guys.

But if we had to write our own Ten Top Tips (eleven, actually!), they'd go like this.

**3. Learn about your life** Is having 'stuff' bad? Not always: trade is not the same as consumption and can support livelihoods. Understand what sustains you and what you need to care about. Learning new talents and skills can help you get there.

**1. Do stuff** Don't waste it, turn it off, turn it down, do it less, do it local, do it yourself, recycle, swap, repair, share.

**4. Increase your reach** There's only so much you can do on your own. Try working with or through other organisations. Also don't forget that your wallet is your weapon. Make buying choices that help good things happen – worldwide.

**2. Be hopeful** Hope isn't just about crossing your fingers. Without it we could get cynical and frozen in despair. Hope is the fuel – but it only works if you do something.

**5. Be angry at the things you can't change** … but think about who can change them. Demand that governments, companies and big organisations change with us and give us real choices.

### 6. Imagine different things

The 21st century will be a time of transformation. Meet different people, explore different things, read different books, try out new ideas.

### 7. Give gifts and give thanks

Understand why we need each other. This is a time to support each other, to work together and build communities.

### 8. Get out more

People can't care about what they don't understand and don't have some sense of connection to. So we need to get out and down in that dirt lest we forget how it keeps us alive. Play together, learn, explore and have adventures.

### 9. Forgive yourself (and others)

Sustainable development will be a territory for endless exploration. Learn from mistakes. We make mistakes because we act, strive and aim high – and that is what makes us human.

### 10. Have fun

'Living a sustainable life' isn't all about 'don't do this' sucking the joy out of living. Where is the adventure in that? There are worlds of possibility out there. Rich cultures, rich experiences, music, laughter, fun and just enjoying life more – foundations for a better future!

### 11. Be the change you wish to see in the world

Gandhi's saying sounds like something from a hippie poster, but actually it was one of the greatest social insights of the 20th century. So, do everything positive you can, not because a list has told you to but because it's who you want to be.

**57**

# The Seasonal Events Programme

This year it's our 10th birthday so we're ramping it up in celebration. Here's a flavour of the sort of things we're doing.

For the latest programme visit **edenproject.com/whats-on**

## Freaky Nature

Discover reality that's so bizarre you couldn't make it up!

## Festival of Play

This summer: dens, music, fire, circus ... playful outdoor activities for all.

Den building

Nofit State Circus

## Halloweden

All things spooky and icy too, as the ice rink returns!

Halloweden

## Our Pollination Team

Bringing you stories and adventures all year round.

*A Time of Gifts*

*Skating*

# A Time of Gifts

Winter festival with ice skating, music, processions, storytelling, markets and workshops.

A time to remember and give thanks for the things we give each other and the natural resources that nurture us.

## Ticketed events

**Eden Sessions** See **edensessions.com** for bands and full details. For priority tickets join our Inside Track Membership.

*Eden Sessions*

## Party time

Some for adults, some for all and some just for the kids.

## Events and hospitality

And of course you can also hire Eden for your very own special event. **edenproject.com/hire**

*Party time*

59

# Where has the money come from?

The Millennium Commission weighed in with £37.5m of lottery funding to single Eden out as the 'landmark' project of the far South West, and their subsequent contributions brought the total to just over £56m. We hope we've delivered for them and for anyone who ever bought a lottery ticket. Other major sources of funding included the EU and Southwest Regional Development Agency (some £50m between them) and £20m of commercial loans. The balance was made up of other loans and some funds generated by Eden itself and reinvested back into the Project.

Maintaining a strong and diverse financial base is crucial to preserving the Eden Trust's independence and credibility. A full list of all our funders to date can be found at **edenproject.com/thankyous**. Thank you.

| How much? | £m |
| --- | --- |
| Buying a large and unusual site, car parks, roads and paths | 16 |
| Reshaping the ground to make it safe, dry and useful | 8 |
| A couple of decent greenhouses | 25 |
| 40 acres of plants … some tall | 3 |
| 83,000 tonnes of manufactured soil to grow them in | 2 |
| A nursery to practise in and grow some unusual plants | 1 |
| Buildings for you and our team – fully equipped | 22 |
| Services to keep it all running | 7 |
| Paying the team up to opening | 3 |
| Exhibits to entertain you, walkways to keep you dry, a lift, a bridge | 12 |
| Advice on the things we couldn't do ourselves | 12 |
| Investments in our future like the Foundation building | 9 |
| A spectacular home for education – The Core | 16 |
| Warehouse, gatehouse, waste compound, Arena | 4 |
| Dreams cost money | Total 140 |

# Be involved

Eden is a charity and our work and successes are only possible thanks to the generosity of our donors, supporters and volunteers. **edenproject.com/support**

## You can support our work in many ways

**Visit us** You're helping just by being here – all the profits from your visit go to the Eden Trust.

**Gift Aid your admission fee** This allows us to claim 25p back from the taxman on every pound you give.

**Become an Eden Friend** You can help us in our work and enjoy benefits too. For full details go to:

- **edenproject.com/friends**
- the Friends information points (see site maps)
- 01726 811932
- **friends@edenproject.com**

**Make a donation** **edenproject.com/donations**
The money we raise goes towards our work on public and formal education, research, conservation and sustainable futures.

**Volunteer** **edenproject.com/volunteer**
Can you spare at least 6 hours a fortnight? Feel good, learn things, meet people – what's not to love? An ideal way to become involved in the daily work of the Project.

**Register for our newsletter**
**edenproject.com/newsletter**

## Useful numbers

General enquiries: 01726 811911 Box office: 01726 811972
Group bookings: 01726 811903  School bookings: 01726 811913

The Eden Project, Bodelva, St Austell, Cornwall PL24 2SG
The Eden Project is a registered charity no. 1093070

**Contact us** **edenproject.com/contact-us**

First published 2001 by Eden Project Books, a division of Transworld Publishers
Eleventh revised edition 2011

Text and design © the Eden Project/Transworld Publishers 2011

Text by Dr Jo Elworthy with assistance from the Eden team

Transworld Publishers, 61–63 Uxbridge Road, London W5 5SA,
a division of the Random House Group Ltd

**booksattransworld.co.uk/eden**

ISBN 9781905811663

Editor: Mike Petty  Design: Charlie Webster  Printed in Great Britain

**MIX**
Paper from
responsible sources
FSC™ C023561

The Eden Project is owned by the Eden Trust, registered charity no. 1093070
and all monies raised go to further the charitable objectives.

Eden Project, Bodelva, St Austell, Cornwall PL24 2SG
T: +44 (0)1726 811911  F: +44 (0)1726 811912
**edenproject.com**

This project is
part-financed by
the European Union
Working with Objective One

The Objective One Partnership
for Cornwall & the Isles of Scilly

South West *of* England
Regional Development Agency

Supported by
**The National Lottery®**
through the Millennium Commission

Millennium Commission

# Rainforest Biome

**Tropical South America**

R.05

R.06 · R.07 · R.08 · R.09

**Crops**

R.11

R.10

R.02

**West Africa**

R.04

**Malaysia**

R.03

**Tropical Islands**

R.12 · R.13 · R.14 · R.15 · R.16

R.19 · R.18 · R.17

R.20 · R.21 · R.22 · R.23

R.01

**Size:** 240m long, 110m wide, 50m high, 15,590m² **Plants:** Over 1,100 different species and cultivars **Temperature:** ranges from 18°C to 35°C **Comfort:** Seats and drinking water fountains throughout and a cool room in West Africa (H.04) for emergencies.